The Battle

Evelyne Weeks

The Battle

A Poetry Collection

Hamilton Cole

Orlando

Published by Hamilton Cole
a subsidiary of studyhorse productions, LLC
Orlando, Florida

Grateful acknowledgment is made to the editors of the following publications, in which the poems listed previously appeared: *The Hollins Critic,* "Appalachia Day 1" (December 1993); *Appalachian Heritage,* "Icicles," "Cowpaths" (Winter 1995); *Out of the Rough: Women's Poems of Survival and Celebration,* "Appalachia Day 1"(2001); *Mountain High,* "On the North Holston" (2008); *You Gotta Love 'em,* "Redbird" (2009); *Traveling Time,* "A Woman Grounded" (2010); *Old Time Mountain Music: A Poetry and Prose Anthology,* "Shoot A Mile" (2011); *Words,* "Straight Edges"(2011)

Cover photography by JoMarie Crews

ISBN 978-0615624730

In memory of my parents,
Jo and Ken Weeks

Contents

Part 1

From every farm there is a church within
walking distance, and a swimming hole.

Cowpaths

Order struck deep grooves in
mountains, rivers, valleys,
spilling yesterday into tomorrow
with little remorse.
An ebb and flow of landscape,
a quilter's hand changing direction—
constant movement to silence
save the still rushing water
over rocks, the hushed dance of
leaves on wind, the too too
quiet sound of land resting, waiting.

Birth and Death balanced like
short and tall against the mountain
where cows made neat paths
winding up slowly and then
turning abruptly to rise
the other way. Hard-packed
well-worn paths, these cow roads
made order questionable,
without physics
to explain rise and slope,
left a child to reason that
even cows grow bored
with going one direction.

Church

Running barefoot between
rows of potato vines
thick with lightning bugs,
the early evening curtain,
and the soft coolness
of dirt between our toes,
we are gathered here—
the two or more—
in reverence.

Called to the dusk
of a bright moon
unleashed this night
to light the world
and the choir,
the katydids howl
rhythm poured pure
into the night,
and the whippoorwill
trades notes with a bullfrog.

The river spills its way south
falling over rocks
into little circle swirls
of instant whirlpools
as fog begins to lift
away the gentle spray.
The night goes dark
and damp, the air cools,
the service ends,
and in a muted chorus
this world gives thanks.

Redbird

The snow is whitest
where a redbird sits
outside my kitchen window,
alone. Red courage puffed up
does more than black
for fat black, black birds
that come in brigades
to this spot in summer
or gold on copper-breasted robins
that eat from the same
worm family in spring.

I'll wear red when I grow up,
stand alone in the
middle of life's avalanche
and never be afraid.
On tip toes, elbows perched
on the counter top,
I take lessons as
outside my kitchen window
a redbird cocks his head.

The Field

In spring, it is well-turned soil—
powdered dirt for running through
barefooted, flat out, hard into the wind
just tilled rows erasing summer past
and there is born a beach.
Mountain air takes on the smell
of oceans for a time.
Then tractors, with a single sweep,
bring changes to this field.
Fill it up with green
and make of it a forest
where knights on horses ride.
And we hang scarves from paper cones
to pin up on our heads and stand
between the even rows—
the plants a cheering crowd
that separates to let us pass,
to view the joust as we were born
to view, with tilted chins
and eyes cast down, alas.
But summer rains change things again.
Leave us with a jungle
where we carry sticks for spears
to fight off anaconda that slither here
beneath the wide dark leaves
that with each day change their shape
and so this field
and so this world.
Till we tie scarves around our necks
and walk the rows from end to end
and worry that the crop won't make
unless it rains again and winter
will be hard this year
according to the signs.

We sip, beneath a sycamore,
lukewarm water from mason jars
and wonder if a sharecropper's part
will feed a clan of nine. But then
mothers' voices change this place
the most and make of it a plain old field
that we wash off and leave behind
for a chance to go to town.
At harvest, workers turn this land
into a desert or a plain or a meadow
dressed in winter rye and we don't run again
till spring brings back the softened earth,
sunbaked and plowed up fine.
Then we go back to children's work
and labor in this field.

On the North Holston

A river front and
a mountain back
and in between
a hundred-year-old house
surrounded by trees as old
to shade the two stories
and shield the tin roof
against occasional sun.

My universe had edges
shaped by God.
The river's other bank,
the mountain's farthest cliff,
and the place where those two met
some distance way off yonder
where some other universe began.
The fourth side opened to the outside,
the only place a surveyor's eye
had ever tinkered with my world.

The old wooden cattle gap
at the end of the drive
was my barrier
to a host of unwelcome guests.
It made it impossible
for demons to come in
or for evil spirits
to pass through and
all scary beasts of the night
dared not cross over
the gapped spaces
that someone long years before
had placed at the end of my drive
to keep the bad things out,
to keep the magic in.

Luck

I found a clover patch
that leafed in four
on every stem,
and I collected them,
one or two at a time
to press in a book
and gave the luck away
when friends would come.
But I never let them look
upon the plant
or to know the secret spot
or that there was just one.

Morning Glories

I watch morning glories
go climbing, vine-tight
up stalks of corn till,
too much trouble to tear down,
like Queen Anne's lace
in fence rows
or thistles in the
belly of a ditch,
they scheme at night to
steal a bit of sun, seize
the first drops of rain and
give memory to forgotten spaces.

So walking home from school
is a picture in the spring
of scrappy little flowers
and scrappy little children
that go on climbing
where they're not wanted
because no one takes the time
to stop them. And there,
while no one's watching,
they make a place to bloom.

Moving Appalachia

Rain in summer, Robber Baron,
wills the earth to move
and valleys slip away.
Rivers warm, take fever,
shudder and muddy.

Water's easy motion
gives way to chaos
as if to cough up phlegm
of banks too early passed
into the natural order.
Measured falls break to run
rush to be rid of trespassers
to separate hot from cool
and empty out the
churning bits of mountains.

Brown water rides past river walls
on to places south
where hay's been baled and
clear flat land spreads out
to welcome it.
And there my valley
lives awhile, till wind,
Seductress, tempts it on
with gifts of flight,
to hotter, dryer spots.

And roads fill up
like rivers do and
folks drift away in little bits
till all my valley's gone—
gone somewhere else to live.

Part 2

People who live their whole lives in the
mountains have a kind of calm about them that
almost seems magic.

A Blackberry Patch

When a woman named Cleo
takes me berry picking,
she carries a stick
and pokes about for snakes
that wait in the briars
for the birds,
then bends the thorny branch
close so I can reach
the sweetest, blackest fruit.
I should learn from this,
the greater bounty
comes with care,
needs a strategy, or
another's helping hand.
But I can't take it in,
here where the question
stops me cold,
on the side of a hill,
wearing boots too big
in a berry patch.
Why would a snake
want to eat a bird?
All feet and feathers
and sharp-pointed beak.
Not easy to swallow.
Why take the egg
still in its shell?

Shoot A Mile

"Shoot a mile, Yes!"
meant something then.
Like mud sliding on mountains,
it would glide down the moment
of our hillbilly tongues
in a rhythm we lived
between hollers and hills
until "mile" was stretched
into tomorrow and "yes"
slapped fast and hard
against a limestone cliff.
We understood Friday night football,
ate chinky pins in school,
and "Shoot a mile, yes!"
we dreamed.

We dreamed of the moon
while men walked there
and so too could we,
on hot summer nights,
but for the swings
behind the school—our birches—
that let us fly up and close,
then stole us back again
just short of mountain lift off.
We went there anyway
on clumsy, cautious first kisses
and celebrated the cusp of
our adulthood amid talk of
impeaching a president
as draft cards lost their meaning.
And, Shoot a mile, yes!
we dreamed.

The eye takes as its purpose the
collection of light

Straight Edges

I like the squared-up line
of words against a margin,
an edge to press against
when poems are born,
where statues want to be.
I dream of sculpting.
I'd like to chisel,
to take away
instead of building up.
The world's so full of clutter.
Yet, till I have eyes to see
the beauty inside a clod
of rock or wood or words,
I'll have to pile it neat
and stand the ink
upright and straight
along a squared-up line.

A Woman Grounded
(after taking back her wings)

I'm done with travel,
like apple picking, now.
I'll give up my pass to board,
let the plane go off without me,
not worry if it's late nor care
what seat, window or aisle or
front or back or even where
it lands. No place is close
enough to here.

And here is where I'll stop.
Trying, pushing, pleasing,
spinning dream lives like
fancy fairy tales for maidens
that surely I was never made to be.
I'll arrive fully formed in the
morning of my own making,
having slept it half away
by my permission.
And since I've thrown out rushing,
I'll be right on time.

In July

And in July
The days are fat
in bloom, and bugs
go lazy-drunk through
drawn-out sunned up days.

I count it twice
so sure the earth
has slowed its turn
and filled my valley
up to brim with life.

I taste in my mind
the sweet stretch
of daylight playing
hopscotch with the clouds,

And hear the rush
of the river
through the open
windows where curtains
dance the days.

Then for a week
or even two
the river warms
just enough to swim.

Icicles

No place grows an icicle
quite like a big tin roof
that wields its power
through the night to
layer, layer, fatter, longer
magic in my morning-gloved hand.

A thing like Merlin knew
but better still, shaped
in ice to extend my reach,
my body's length
yet clear through
like shiny glass and
as dangerous
at right angles,
stabbed just so.

No hand-forged knife
centuries old with mystic power
could ever cast a spell so strong
to send the bearer off through time
to dragonslay or kingdomsave
and then get used up,
the fuel of play
that drips away
to round the world
and land another icy night
on some other roof of tin.

The Battle

I remember crocus
just at the top of the walk
to either side, one right, one left
patient soldiers standing guard
waiting to war with winter.
Like tiny Davids
stubby, chubby thick-like limbs
lash out at snow through frozen ground
just there down low
where even children have to kneel
to watch the power in the stems
that know just when
the battle-weary wind
will succumb to bravery or mad lust.
The crocus seems full up with both.
And on they come in sweet duet,
sing out "wake-up" to daffodils
and hyacinth near who wait for sun.
But these prophets know the coming
of the stretched-out measure of the day,
so on they climb and fight off ice
to stir the souls of those who
helpless watch the tiny buds,
the cloudy skies fluffed up with snow.
This, this is such a show
for eyes that stop to stare
at purple petals, tiny violet flowers
rising up out of the last gasp of winter
to mock the cold, the shortened day
and with perfect faith
turn faces up to greet
the golden turn of heaven.

Appalachia Day 1

We came to this place
in the night,
amid stories of bears
and mountain lions,
to enormous ceilings
dark dusty wood
and the cobwebs of ghost stories.
To say goodbye
to ocean air forever,
ignored for its constant presence
replaced with pungent breezes
heavy with November coal stove smoke.

Too young to understand
the way geography
will slice a life like butter
and change the shape of things
until they can never be reshaped
the way they were before
when life had not yet felt
the strain of massive chunks of
land piled in upon
all that is comfortable,
I did not feel the sting of goodbye.

I was the youngest
and followed the rest
to this new mountain home
that I could not imagine.
There is no pain in the first real goodbye.

Part 3

In the early, learning years, it matters who, or what, is doing the teaching.

Every child keeps a diary in his head; some get read more than others

Frogs and Such

It was a tree frog
that first shattered equilibrium
stood the world on its head
for all its reason—sure and constant
cycles in practiced returning seasons,
Summer into Fall and all around
a purpose and a place and a time
and then, a frog, in my Granny's
front yard, in a tree.

Lilypad-less creatures
melding with the night and
singing notes impossible to describe
like croaks of river banks'
fat-bellied bulls that plop into the water
with a sound that explodes against
the quiet stillness of the dark.

I've claimed a frog or two
along the way and seen up close
the knotted-up thickness of their hides,
the lumpy nature of their being, and
I've measured them beside
the smoothness of a tree frog in the
gentlest shade of green whose
seamless body is covered
shiny tight in perfect flawless skin.

And I go back again to equilibrium,
the balance of it all or lack
and give hours to the effort
of making sense of things, when
frogs in trees all but lead me to
throw up hands and give in to happenstance.

But my teacher is the river
and teaches long and well—
on days I listen—that being certain
is a mistake and sometimes clouds
don't look like anything to those of us
who think we've seen it all.

And if you were a frog
with suction cups for feet
that made climbing trees seem natural,
there too suppose you chose to go
up among the leaves
for little better reason
than that you knew you could.

Snow

When snow has snowed a winter full
and still it snows
in blinding sheets
long past its welcome,
beyond its due,
then children, tired of it,
wear boots to church on Easter
hide pastels under winter coats
and long to look like catalog kids
with tulip baskets and broad-brimmed hats.

But heaven's turned its back on us
and chocolate rabbits fail
to explain resurrection
in Sunday school.
Under inches of ice
the river gurgles,
slows down like dying
and still it snows.
Our Savior freezes to death,
rolls back the stone against
the frozen ground,
while spring is still asleep.

Steam rises from newborn calves
struggling to stand
against the wind,
thick, heavy flakes
muffle their cries
and punish their early births.
Corn cribs empty, haylofts echo,
coal piles dwindle to pebble rings,
the world flattens out,
and still it snows.

Farmers round the stove at Harve's
learn that Boo Johnson in Possum Holler
still has hay for sale.

Mr. Henry's losing sheep,
too many orphaned lambs to nurse.
He sings "Old Rugged Cross,"
every verse, without a hymnal.
In Sunday school
we think they've got it wrong.
Jesus wears sandals
in our picture books.
And still it snows.

On Memory

I've lied it seems,
not meaning to
and mostly to myself,
that going back
is finding things
just the way they were.

That rivers hold
a constant depth
and shapes eroded there
can not be seen in
just these twenty years.

And stepping barefoot
in the river's edge
on softened sides
of river rocks,
the icy water grabs
my ankle,
a wet slice,
like cold metal
separates the numbed foot
from the warm leg.

So there I mark it
and plan to prove
it's just the same today
as then, at nine,
when I felt the water
grip my foot,
pulling tight
at tendons with
frigid force and
steady, relentless motion.

But the water's not as
cold or deep and
the willow tree
is gone from there
on the bank
where you and I would sit.

Maple Trees

Maple trees are born with wings,
fill the sky at birthing time
with thupt thupt thupt
helicopter imitations
to delight grounded little girls
whose necks grow tired
from peering up in hopes to spot
the limb turn loose its winged child.

Young seeds sail past
the crashing birth of oaks,
the clumsy, too big, beginnings
of sycamores and walnuts,
beyond kidnapping squirrels
and murderous birds to vanity
spawned of privileged birth.

To grow up and dress
in gaudy colors and flaunt
their leaves cross ground and sky.
Prideful limbs with perfect posture
stretch their way to heaven,
commune with clouds and moon
and rarely dip to bend toward earth.

My house was fronted with
these snobby regal trees
throwing piles of yellow and orange
with striking red across my sloping
front yard playground.
They were loud trees with
lovely leaves and massive trunks,
firmly planted, almost laughing,
even at the birds.

● ● ●

Water

Clarity comes in the
streams of a spring
that fall from the
mountain to the
tap in my kitchen.
And there I meet
the power
of the steady
relentless push of
the earth's tears
seeping through
fissures carved in
ages of rock,
the art of gravity
dancing with winter,
reined in, but not
fully harnessed.
Each day I bathe in
the mountain,
drink of it
and feel its force.

Courage

I think of worlds
and what they hold
for those who live
inside the little
trough of stillness
that a river rock
might hide.

Beneath the rushing
clearness in the
current's churning
flow, I find a bright
green water snake
tied nearly in a bow.

Hidden safe and
sleeping underneath
a broad flat stone,
until I wander close
enough to see if
someone's home.

For just a time
we freeze right there
each surprised as each,
to at that moment
be troubled by
a meeting such as this.

Just before I
turn to run,
the snake has won
the race and unknots
itself to slide

away to a safer
hiding place.

Then as my heart
slows back to beat
at summer's normal calm,
I see the mess
I've clearly made
by choosing
just this stone.

Still the bravest
thing I do at nine
is face the world
I just might find
if I have guts to
lift a river rock.

Listen

The quiet is unnatural
when the winter
dips deep enough
to freeze the flow
of the river
and ice sculptures form
where water would
spill in tiny falls
over the breadth of rock.

Fat flakes of snow
float down on us
and soundproof
the world until the only
noise I hear
is the crunch
under my own boot.

Granny

In Spring, she will plant tomatoes and marigolds
outside the kitchen window, side by side,
so the one can save the other from the armies of
summer pests that surely will come.

In Summer, she will peel apples for apple butter
and count the fogs in August
then put a bean into the jar to mark
the snows that will fall in winter.

In Autumn, she will supervise the hog-killing,
not let anyone else touch the meat
for fear it won't be cleaned properly,
won't cure out for the holidays ahead.

In Winter, she'll read her Bible,
stay inside to avoid a fall on the ice,
cook huge pots of brown beans,
and late at night, turn her eyes toward heaven
to understand why he is gone.

Part 4

A trip implies I'm coming back,
A journey not as much

Truth

How inadequate a
thing a poem is
next to the green
of a pasture tended
by cattle in spring.

Treasure

Imagination walks with me,
climbs the cow path
to the top of the hill,
carries the heavy load
of end tables and lamps,
heavy drapes and oriental carpet
to fill up the room
of my lovely limestone couch
with its high back
and perfect bench seat.

It fixes the bay window
to arch out over the cliff
and hugs the view below,
welcomes the guests
that have followed us here
to admire the lucky find,
and hides from the cows
when they come too close.

Time

Time floats inside old houses
up and out of chimneys
through open upstairs windows
and lingers too
on sleepy summer days
stretched across pillows
cased in linen
pressed out after
drying in the sun.
Hours shift and bend
until the great metronome
of earth is distracted
and minutes become
whole notes
full and pure and round.
Shadows stop,
become shade,
the sun sits still
and I listen.

Harvest

During a tobacco fall,
the boys leave school
to work the barns,
take the cured leaves
down from drying,
and stack them in
lovely bound bunches
for market and a year's
income for a family.

When they return,
the rich brown stains
on their hands
become a badge
of sorts, of honor
or of shame, that
even now the
crop that kills
will carry them
through winter.

Then I get back
the empty loft—
a place to read
and dream,
filled now with the
fading sweet scent
of tobacco
cured softly
in purest mountain air.

Looking up

It's true that trees
are bone-like bare
before the spring
after the fall
but for the very tops,
the part too far away
to clearly see.
It looks so much like fuzz
I think they all need hats.

I can't remember
who taught me how
to make a blade of grass
whistle, but I am glad

Sounds like Day

Morning gives
back the magic black
of darkest early hour,
throws off the evening
wrap to spring
upon the world
a light so loud
and new
I think I have
first heard.
And hearing this
the certain groan
of tilted earth
against a well-used
hinge, I'm sure I feel
the atoms spill
and break along a
measured fault
in time.

Lilacs

Under the kitchen window
purple blooms upon
a lilac bush that was left
by a woman whose child was grown

Who liked to tend the garden
in the early part of spring
and knew the sweet, sweet fragrance
would intoxicate the bees.

Had seen the way the scent
would cast about like fishing
and lure us young and old
to gather in this spot

To bury noses in great
grape-hanging clusters
to quell the doubt that anything
could smell so surely sweet.

Bees go drunk when the lilacs bloom
and stagger fly around the bush
and bump against the world
with soft apology that does not scare.

Crochet

When I sit with yarn and hook
and count and loop my way along
I like to think I link myself
to those who long ago did much
the same on afternoons when
cold and rain had forced them
in away from outside chores.

But girls who learned the half
back stitch before the age of
nine could surely work filet by ten,
girls who mastered this as I will not,
though I have no stove to stoke
and no butter has been churned

And though I'm grown I
like to play, imagining somehow
my way to times I can not
measure myself beside.
Were their stitches always even?
Did their rows all look the same?

*The river gives direction
to the road...and the world*